SERVICE LED DESIGN

Service Led Design

Planning the New HR Function

Jane Saunders and
Ian Hunter

Routledge
Taylor & Francis Group

LONDON AND NEW YORK

First published 2009 by Gower Publishing

Published 2016 by Routledge
2 Park Square, Milton Park, Abingdon, Oxon OX14 4RN
711 Third Avenue, New York, NY 10017, USA

Routledge is an imprint of the Taylor & Francis Group, an informa business

British Library Cataloguing in Publication Data
Saunders, Jane.
  Service led design : planning the new HR function. -- (The Gower HR transformation series)
  1. Personnel management--Practice.
  I. Title II. Series III. Hunter, Ian, 1963-
  658.3-dc22

Library of Congress Cataloging-in-Publication Data

Saunders, Jane.
  Service led design : planning the new HR function / by Jane Saunders and Ian Hunter.
    p. cm. -- (The Gower HR transformation series)
  Includes index.
  ISBN 978-0-566-08826-1 (pbk) -- ISBN 978-0-7546-8161-8 (ebook)
  1. Personnel management. 2. Strategic planning. I. Hunter, Ian, 1963- II. Title.
  HF5549.S1786 2009
  658.3'01--dc22

                                                                200901150

ISBN 13: 978-0-566-08826-1 (pbk)

Contents

List of Figures   *vii*
List of Tables   *ix*

1   Commercializing HR   1

2   Establishing your HR Service Vision   5

3   Specifying the Service: What Will HR Deliver?   15

4   The Building Blocks: The Service Delivery Model   23

5   Adapting the Model   47

6   New HR – New Line Management?   55

7   Sizing the Operation and Building the Business
     Case   61

8   Managing the Service   69

List of Figures

1.1	The balance and shape of focus in the new HR model	2
2.1	Typical management feedback	9
2.2	What needs to change?	9
2.3	What will the service design principles deliver?	10
2.4	Transport for London – HR service design principles	12
2.5	High-level responsibilities and the focus of the new HR function	13
3.1	Service Specification – an example	19
4.1	Accessing HR – managing your channels	25
4.2	Tiering of service within the SSC	30
4.3	Service tiering summary – scope and delivery mechanisms	41
4.4	Typical HRSSC technology architecture	44
5.1	Service centre distribution – implications for service delivery	48
5.2	Levels of integration	52
6.1	Typical line management accountability	56
6.2	Example – change impact summary	57
6.3	Example – summary impact assessment	58
6.4	Example – what the service means	59
7.1	Components of the business case	63
8.1	Illustrative HR governance framework	71

8.2   Example – Service Management Framework   76
8.3   Outline example of a balanced scorecard
         for HR solutions   78

List of Tables

3.1	What HR should consider in a business led service design	16–17
4.1	Typical Tier self-service transactions	32–33
4.2	Typical Tier 1 transactions	34–35
4.3	Typical Tier 3 transactions	39
7.1	Example ratios for 'sizing' a shared services operation based on Orion Partners client engagements 2002–2008	65

① Commercializing HR

For many years now, both private and public sector organizations have been dealing with the challenges of how best to improve corporate performance. HR has not escaped this scrutiny; the need to establish the function as a business partner has bought the performance of HR into the spotlight and positioned it as a target for transformation in efficiency and effectiveness.

Technology has been the key enabler in re-shaping HR. The level of automation introduced has driven down the previously labour intensive transactional and administrative elements that can account for up to 70 per cent of the time, effort and cost of the traditional HR function. This automation has allowed businesses to focus on the real value-add elements, improving the performance of both the HR function and the business itself.

Those very same businesses that have been spending recent years cost cutting, restructuring and streamlining, are putting the pressure on the HR 'overhead' to prove that it is not just a cost centre, but a function that provides added value through alignment to business needs and aspirations.

The traditional, transaction-based HR service must, however, still be delivered. Understanding how to combine a renewed strategic focus with effective delivery of transactional and administrative services is the key to HR's next generation.

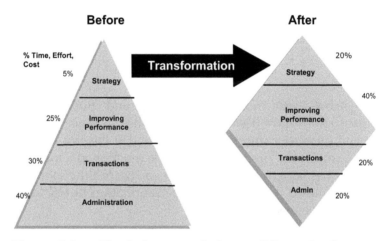

Figure 1.1   The balance and shape of focus in the new HR model

The idea of transforming HR is not new and, over the last ten years, many private and public sector organizations have attempted to reshape their function in this way. There have been success stories. There have also been a number of instances where the transformation has failed to deliver. A number of organizations are still struggling to make the initial vision of a strategic HR function a reality. Why do programmes that are similarly resourced, funded and managed end up with radically different results? What makes the difference between success and failure?

Although the rationale for change may be clear – lower cost and improved service and performance – it is in the initial focus of many HR transformation programmes that long-term problems can begin. Too often, organizations focus attention and effort on those areas that have been seen to deliver change in re-engineering other corporate support functions such as finance and procurement for example:

- Detailed process design;

- Systems functionality;

- Headcount reduction.

While these areas are important, transformation initiatives that have them as their sole focus can fail to consider how the whole HR delivery model will work and, more crucially, fit into the business.

In our work with HR functions, we have established a clear set of criteria and approach that we believe differentiates between a successful implementation and what can be a costly backward step that only serves to alienate the business:

- Define the service the **business** needs;

- Ensure your design is **integrated**;

- Make **intelligent** use of technology;

- **Manage** the change at all levels within the business;

- Establish the **disciplines** to run HR as a business.

(2) Establishing your HR Service Vision

WHAT DOES THE BUSINESS NEED?

To realize the cost and service benefits, both HR and the business it serves must understand exactly what each of them expects from the function and be clear how the new model will change and improve current operations. This means starting at the top and agreeing with key business stakeholders the features of the HR service that will really make a difference to how their business is supported. These features then form a core set of design principles around which the whole solution can be designed and developed.

The first step in achieving an effective design for your HR service is to build a strong understanding of how customers from all around the organization view the current service; establish what it is they value, the gaps they perceive in that service and what they would like to see as outcomes from a new way of working. However, it is at this stage that many organizations fall into the basic trap of allowing the detail of HR process and technology to dictate the outcomes. While technology is a key enabler, it must not be construed as the panacea that will in itself deliver a perfect service. In isolation technology alone will not deliver the improved efficiency and effectiveness that will allow HR to deliver on its strategic agenda. It is simply a tool.

The HR function touches the organization in many different ways. The processes for which it is responsible run at the heart of the relationship between the organization, its current managers and employees, as well as potential or previous employees. It is understanding how these interactions can be most effective, rather than just the process that underpins them, that is most important. Identifying where the gaps are and how best to fill them will provide the basis for a successful implementation and increase the take-up of new ways of working in the business. It is crucial that the organization is given the opportunity to articulate a high level vision of exactly what is needed and valued in order to build a picture of the business outcomes required from a new HR service. There are three key benefits from engaging the business in this way:

1. This initial phase of the design process is at the heart of identifying where the focus of HR should lie. It will help to shape the design in terms of who does what, and where both activity and accountability should lie.

2. By ensuring everyone is involved and is able to see evidence that business input is incorporated into the design of the end solution, buy-in from the organization and the long-term success of the programme is more likely. If this buy-in is not gained and the organization feels that large-scale change is being done *to them* rather than *in partnership with them*, there is a very real risk of corporate disobedience

which will undermine the success of the entire programme before it has even been implemented.

3. The process ensures that the business articulates what it needs; it shapes the transformation's starting point. It naturally builds in an improvement feedback loop with the business into the HR programme. This will make working from initial to final design, through transition and implementation far less problematic than might otherwise be the case. In cases where the organization is involved every step of the way, the final outcome should be exactly what is needed and more readily adopted.

How the business is engaged in this phase of the design process to best effect depends on the type of organization and its individual culture. Ideally, the engagement should have a structured approach and typically involve a series of senior management interviews, with subsequent workshops and focus groups for detailed design and ongoing validation. These interactions are aimed at finding the answer to a small number of simple but important questions:

- What are the challenges facing the organization?

- What is HR's role in meeting these?

- Where should HR focus – in the short, medium and long term?

- What should HR 'stop, start and continue' to deliver?

At times, it can be difficult to resist the temptation of diving straight into people's views on the merits and faults of existing HR processes. However, in starting the debate with a focus on the business outcomes HR needs to deliver, it is possible to get to what is most important for the organization and where the priorities should lie.

In our experience, getting the balance between genuine engagement with the business and the risk of design by committee is important. Identifying the appropriate number and level of people with whom to engage will be determined by the type of organization. The key is that the dialogue is meaningful and seen to be with individuals or groups who are representative of the needs of the organization.

Irrespective of the type of organization, large or small, public or private, there are often many similarities in what different businesses require from their HR functions. At this stage of a programme, it can feel as if this process is an exercise is defining statements of the obvious and that the HR function could simply list the priorities they perceive as important and get ninety-five percent of the way there by themselves. Invariably, the business will want to see improved accessibility, accuracy and a service that supports managers. At the same time they are likely to want a service that drives performance through the line and holds them accountable for managing their people. However, the key is that these requirements are articulated in the language of the organization so that it resonates well and has impact. It is as much a step in the change management journey as it is an exercise in requirements definition – but miss it at your peril!

Figure 2.1 illustrates the contributions from HR that an organization typically values.

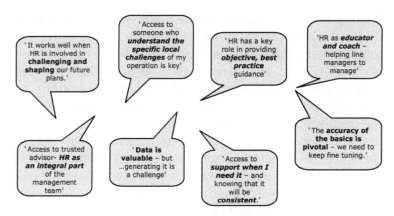

Figure 2.1   Typical management feedback

And this is how HR service delivery may need to change as a result. (Figure 2.2)

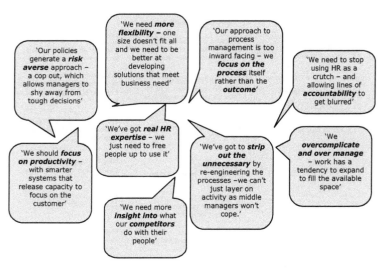

Figure 2.2   What needs to change?

Starting with the business' service requirements, rather than the underlying process, ensures that the model delivers a solution that will be used, rather than one that just services the needs of HR. Well articulated in clear language that everyone understands, these principles will form the touchstone to which the HR function can return to keep them honest. When the complexities of running the change programme begin to blur the original business objectives, checking back against these original design principles is a very useful discipline. If these principles are clear from the outset, organizations will avoid one of the most common causes of failure; disconnection between the business and HR.

Figure 2.3 shows how the original senior stakeholder input to the design principles translates to key messages and the desired business outcomes that support them.

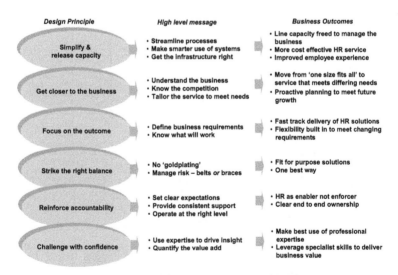

Design Principle	High level message	Business Outcomes
Simplify & release capacity	• Streamline processes • Make smarter use of systems • Get the infrastructure right	• Line capacity freed to manage the business • More cost effective HR service • Improved employee experience
Get closer to the business	• Understand the business • Know the competition • Tailor the service to meet needs	• Move from 'one size fits all' to service that meets differing needs • Proactive planning to meet future growth
Focus on the outcome	• Define business requirements • Know what will work	• Fast track delivery of HR solutions • Flexibility built in to meet changing requirements
Strike the right balance	• No 'goldplating' • Manage risk – belts or braces	• Fit for purpose solutions • One best way
Reinforce accountability	• Set clear expectations • Provide consistent support • Operate at the right level	• HR as enabler not enforcer • Clear end to end ownership
Challenge with confidence	• Use expertise to drive insight • Quantify the value add	• Make best use of professional expertise • Leverage specialist skills to deliver business value

Figure 2.3   What will the service design principles deliver?

CASE STUDY

SEEING DESIGN PRINCIPLES USED IN ACTION – TRANSPORT FOR LONDON

In 2003, the HR leadership of Transport for London (TfL) embarked on a far reaching programme to transform their HR function. The HR needs of the business had previously been met by multiple HR departments, each supporting the individual companies and business units which had originally made up the complex structure of the transportation provider. Although TfL had been officially created in 2000, the notion of an integrated organization was still somewhat theoretical and it was not until 2003 that the real work of post-merger integration began in earnest.

Senior executive engagement and buy-in was the first of a number of key principles that TfL got right from the outset and which were key to the success of the transformation programme.. The driving forces behind the programme were already clear:

- Service improvement;
- Integrated delivery;
- Post merger synergy and efficiency.

The high level blueprint of a shared services delivery model had already been agreed in principle, with a vision for a leading-edge shared service centre to manage HR operations and the introduction of HR Business Partner teams within each of the organization's major business units. However taking this from a theoretical model for service delivery to a new way of doing business required a catalyst to bring the process to life. This was achieved through a relatively simple and straightforward engagement exercise. It involved the Programme Director discussing the service requirements of each of the businesses with their respective

11

directors to gain a clear view on both the business and HR priorities that would shape the design of the new HR service. The outputs of these discussions were distilled down and the following statements agreed as the principles that would underpin the transformation programme.

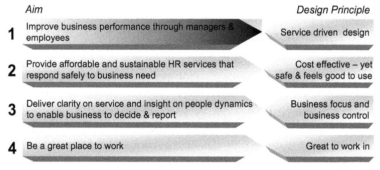

Figure 2.4   Transport for London – HR service design principles

Their practical application was critical and is best illustrated by taking a concrete example. The first principle was based on the need to mark a real shift in both the cultural attitude towards and the ownership of performance management. Historically TfL did not have a strong culture of performance management. As in many public sector organizations, there was a sense that 'time served' was what counted rather than outputs delivered. The management of employee performance was also seen as something that HR was responsible for 'sorting out' and management were easily able to abdicate responsibility for taking the right actions. Making a clear statement that business performance was to be improved through managers and employees was critical to defining the role that HR would take. It was about empowering these groups to undertake their responsibilities through the provision of a consistent and responsive service, rather than executing these activities on their behalf.

THE HR OPERATING MODEL

With a clear vision of what HR needs to deliver in place, you can begin to assess what kind of operating model will need to be put in place. At the most simple level, you should be looking at delivering transactional and administrative services in the most efficient and least labour intensive way. You should also examine the most effective way of providing strategic level advice and support for business improvements. A typical model, shown in Figure 2.5, will see these activities and accountabilities split between a Shared Service Organization (SSO), specialist Centres of Expertise (CoE) and HR Business Partners (HRBP) with the HR Leadership setting the overall agenda.

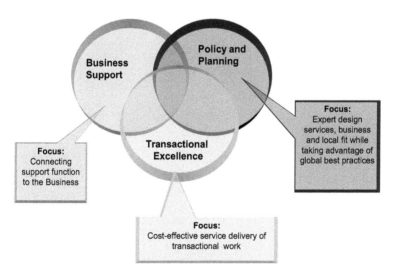

Figure 2.5   **High-level responsibilities and the focus of the new HR function. Orion Partners 2006**

This outline model has proved successful in many organizations but the relative size, shape and focus of the component parts can differ significantly. HR's challenge is working out how the model in Figure 2.5 should be developed to fit within an individual corporate context. Getting this fit right is fundamental to the transformation's success and in detail it is never the same for any two businesses, even if they are in the same sector or have similar workforce profiles.

With a clear set of design principles, it is HR's job to build the model around what the business values and needs. We will examine the individual building blocks of the model in more detail in Chapter 4, but the next step in the process is about taking the high level vision of the required service vision and initial views on the target operating model and bringing this to life.

3 Specifying the Service: What Will HR Deliver?

WHAT SERVICES WILL HR DELIVER?

It is at this point in the design process that many organizations move straight from high-level vision into detailed process mapping. In our experience, this approach is where the service focus can get lost and result in a design driven more on the basis of making HR more efficient rather than ensuring that it will deliver the right service to the business. It is important for the HR function and its parent organization to start thinking of the function in a different way. HR is not just a set of processes underpinned by useful technology. It is the intelligent interpretation and application of these processes to address the business' needs that will deliver great service.

The key here is to think in terms of providing the best possible customer experience to line managers and employees. Although the concept of the internal customer may seem hackneyed and overused, it is one that HR has been slow to grasp. We have often found it somewhat of a challenge to get

HR professionals to put themselves in the shoes of their internal customers and focus on their needs rather than starting from the viewpoint of HR process and policy. If HR starts with the customer in mind, there are some fundamental questions that can be asked. If these are considered from a business context, as shown in Table 3.1, this will provide a much more rounded perspective on the design.

Table 3.1   What HR should consider in a business led service design. Orion Partners 2008

Question to HR	Design considerations for the business
Who are your customers?	Do all parts of the organization need/want the same service? How homogenous are current processes, systems, and procedures? How important is geographical/local knowledge?
What services do they require?	What are the business priorities? What should be the balance of shared vs. local service delivery? Are some services relevant to specific businesses and less easy to leverage? Is an enterprise model (for example, multi functional including Finance and Procurement an option?
How is current service perceived?	Will they be resistant to change? Could current service issues be 'quick wins' for implementation
How will they access services?	What is your contact management strategy – click/call/face? What are the technology implications? What is the level of line manager capability/confidence?

Table 3.1 *Concluded*

How will they pay?	What do they value? What is the balance between cost and quality? How will services be costed and charged – cost recovery, usage based charging?
How might their needs change?	How do you build flexibility into the service? How do you assess and cater for future capacity requirements? What are the technology implications?

When the processes required to deliver the full lifecycle of HR service from attraction of talent through to exit management are analysed, an inventory of between one hundred and fifty and two hundred discrete processes is not untypical. The prospect of testing all two hundred in detail can be overwhelming, and though this effort will be needed when the detailed design phase begins, a dose of pragmatism is what is required at the outset. In our experience, the most effective way to ensure that service design process delivers the service required is to start by identifying a core set of priority processes that can then be designed and refined in detail. A useful set of criteria for selecting these is as follows:

- Volume – what are the highest volume processes that require significant manpower to deliver?

- Business Impact – which processes are critical in your business? These will differ by organization and be driven by the kind of business you are in for example, high seasonal recruitment pressures in leisure or retail, performance management in professional services or compliance issues in banking and insurance.

- Technology dependent – which processes are likely to have the most significant demands from a technology perspective?

Applying these criteria typically results in organizations identifying between fifteen and twenty processes that can then be modelled so that a real understanding of how services could be delivered in the future can be achieved. This modelling allows the HR function to get a clear picture of where accountability for delivery might sit and how activities will be organized. It also allows them to begin testing this with the business in a way that delivers an initial view of the change impact, and also builds on the initial engagement around the service vision.

We sometimes refer to this as the service specification or service proposition. In practical terms, this stage of the design process requires working through the priority processes from end-to-end; in other words, starting from the customer perspective and then identifying what will be required to achieve the desired outcome. The service specification allows the different players in the delivery of the HR service to see who is responsible for what and also to see how services will be accessed – for example, electronically via self service, over the phone or face to face (Figure 3.1).

The service specification is a very useful format through which to test the validity of the initial design principles. Further detail is obviously required to map all the individual processes when design progresses to the level of detailed systems requirements definition – but at this stage it provides a robust assessment

Service category	I need to...	I will need to go on-line for...	I will then need to...	Shared Services will...	HR Mgt will...	Employee will...	Senior manager will...	Central teams will...
External Recruitment (specialist or one off vacancy)	Recruit a specialist or one off vacancy	Basic advice about recruiting a specialist or one off vacancy To get refresher training in any part of the process Ensure I have sufficient numbers of recruiters in my team Request placement of external advert(s) and find out data to populate this Raise vacancies in HR application, providing the relevant contractual data and submit request for any necessary authorizations Ensure the HR system knows my recruiter(s), their availability and job data Review my schedule/that of my recruiters to see when assessments are booked Review my schedule to see when essessments are booked	Talk to HR Shared Services if I have more detailed questions/am unclear on process of recruiting a specialist or one off vacancy Check original eligibility documentation matches the photocopy and that it is clear, and scan/send these to SS for eligibility checks Conduct assessments Make selection decisions, accept/reject candidates and place them to vacancies online Offer the individual the position with support from SS Provide SS with expect advice on where they may be able to source a specific applicant or skills base/who to target	Implement a specific attraction campaign using appropriate 3rd party if necessary Produce the documentation to support the process Provide the vacancy owner and/or recruiter with CV and/or applicant data prior to the assessment Partner the vacancy owner through a Specialist Campaign to offer a high touch consistent service Allocate interviewers and line manager of recruitment event/assessment Conduct pre-screening and eligibility checks Corporate evaluation and monitoring of eligibility to work Offer management where the campaign/vacancy owner has agreed this upfront, in the format agreed Administer offer letters and copy to Line Manager Conduct post assessment administration inc. Contract etc. Assign the individual to Induction Set up new employee Personal Files Maintain Organization Structure Provide me with the advice I need or brief a specialist to contact me for very specialist positions Research and recommend benchmarking for specialist position to Central Team	Review local MI and succession plans Support build of Business Case for specialist position Support with assessments of specialist position	Make application via agency if appropriate Submit CV and/or relevant data to SS Access vacancies online Access vacancies by phone to Shared Services Apply online or by phone Attend assessment Bring originals of eligibility to work documentation plus photocopies	Review actual salary bill data vs. targets in line with recruitment campaigns Review actual recruitment numbers and cost in line with target recruitment numbers and cost Review MI data ref; vacancy fulfilment vs. plan Support and build business case to central team for exception role Authorize vacancy Authorize exception role to blueprint and benchmarking	Define policy Provide advice to experts within Shared Services on exceptional/unique situations Review MI

Figure 3.1 Service Specification- an example. Orion Partners 2007

of how the operating model would work in delivering the HR service. For best results, we advocate a three-step process:

1. Draft the specification – work with a core team of representatives from the HR team to develop a 'starter for ten' which you can then test in a number of working sessions.

2. The HR Review – review the proposed service designs with the HR teams. Ask them to review the services from several perspectives. These are:

    -   *Supply* – typically the HR operations/administration and specialist teams who are focused on how key HR processes will be delivered
    -   *Demand* – HR generalists from the business who are focused on how well the proposed services will meet line manager and employee needs

3. The Customer Review – review the proposed services with representatives from the customer base. The review should accommodate any differences in workforce profile. For example if you are undertaking the exercise within a local government organization, it is important for the teams to understand the wide range of requirements for dealing with a user base that includes head teachers and social workers, care assistants, town planners and many others. It is also important that the proposed services are fully reviewed from both the line manager and employee perspective as their needs will differ.

Bringing the model to life in this way has a number of benefits. Although the changes that need to occur when moving from a traditional HR model are easy to grasp at a conceptual level, it is often only when the specifics of how the model will work in practice are really explored that the organization begins to understand what this will mean for roles and responsibilities and for skills and capabilities. As well as testing the model for operational fit, this phase of the design process also allows an early view of the scale of organizational change required which is particularly helpful when assessing what level of investment will be required to help manage the transformation.

The Building Blocks: The Service Delivery Model

Once the initial service vision is agreed and a high level view of how core processes will be delivered is understood, it is time to develop the detail of the operating model. It is at this stage that a detailed picture of what activities will sit where will fully emerge and the real shape of the new HR function will start to become clear.

CHANNEL MANAGEMENT

Decisions about the channels that will be used to access HR should be finalized at this point in the design process. In due course, these channels will drive the requirements for the technology needed to support the service. The split of 'click vs. call vs. face' will be driven by the culture of the organization, its technology orientation as well as its geographical complexity. A new model should introduce improved efficiencies and effectiveness for HR services by standardising the approach across the whole business to make the most of economies of both scale and skill.

To achieve the benefits of introducing a new approach to HR, it is important that all activities are scrutinized to establish where each specific activity within a given process best fits. For example, it may make far more sense for a line manager to take responsibility for entering data such as records of absence or information regarding appraisals and pay into the HR system. Directly involving HR and sending paper forms around the organization will elongate the process, both in terms of number of steps and in time to completion, and introduces the risk of human error. It is these kinds of activities that may well be best delivered through the introduction of self service technology – Employee Self Service (ESS) and Manager Self Service (MSS). However, decisions on the appropriateness of this will be determined by a range of factors – including accessibility to technology, work patterns and so on.

With more complex HR processes, such as managing a complex disciplinary problem or grievance, it is access to the right technical expertise at the point of need that is critical. In this scenario, providing line managers with swift access to specialist help will be key in the design of how queries of this kind are escalated through the frontline service agents (in a shared services operation) to specialist case worker teams. The simple principles to apply are that from a transactional perspective, changes to process should primarily involve standardization that saves time, effort and duplication across HR, line management and employees. From the value-added perspective, changes should mean that the right people with the right skill sets are focused at the right level on the work for which they are most suitable. Figure 4.1 illustrates how queries might typically be distributed across the levels of expertise within the HR functions and how these services may be accessed from on-line at level 1 through to face-to-face at level 4.

Traditionally, many HR employees would have been generalists, with their day-to-day role split across administration, transactional activity, case work and strategy. The old adage of jack of all trades and master of none can be an appropriate one. Not only is this an inefficient use of resource, it limits the ability to make best use of the available skills and will dilute the quality of service provision. However, many HR professionals have relished the variety that the generalist role brings and this can be a challenge if individuals perceive that a move to segmenting skills and services may narrow the role.

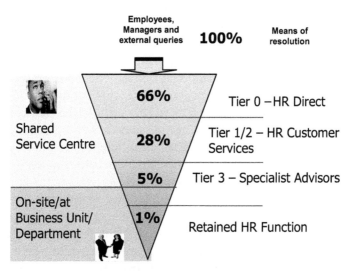

Figure 4.1   Accessing HR – managing your channels. Orion Partners 2008

At this point it is appropriate to examine each part of the model in detail. Each component of the HR function has a clearly defined role. The success of the model relies on the integration between the component parts – resulting in seamless service delivery to the business.

THE HR LEADERSHIP TEAM

In Figure 2.5 we provided a high level overview of the different roles and responsibilities within the HR function. Key to the effectiveness of the overall model is the HR Leadership team. Providing direction for the HR function as a whole, the HR Leadership team ensures that the business is translating corporate HR policy and strategic direction correctly and that they are fully supported by the HR function. Governance for the whole HR model will also rest with this group of individuals, ensuring that HR is following best practice, delivering what it should be and remaining closely integrated with the business. The group will typically be made up of the senior representatives from each of three main components of the function – Business HR, Shared Services and the Centres of Expertise/Excellence. Reporting lines may vary by organization; they may all be to the HR Director, but there may also be some cases where the primary reporting lines are into the executive team of the business area supported. Even where this is the case, there should still be a tight relationship between senior HR figures in the business and the HR Leadership team as alignment around what HR is there to achieve at this level is critical. It is the behaviours of this team that will set the tone for the rest of the function and it is from here that the value added to the business by HR should be articulated.

HR BUSINESS PARTNERS

It is the role of the HR Business Partner (HRBP) to provide the strategic interface between the business and HR. Individuals in these roles will not typically get involved in the delivery of day-to-day HR activity. They should be part of senior management in the area in which they operate and it is their role to articulate (for the benefit of the HR function) what the business needs are and be the advocates of HR back to the business. The role is an analytical one that requires a deep understanding of the business and the part that HR can play in ensuring medium and long-term objectives are met.

The HRBPs need to work with their senior management to ensure that people planning becomes a natural constituent of the business' planning cycle . This will ensure that the organization's objectives and long-term aspirations are supported by a meaningful people strategy. Identifying the skills that will be needed and ensuring that the appropriate strategies are in place to attract, build and retain the right talent is a key focus of the HRBP role.

CENTRE OF EXPERTISE/EXCELLENCE

The Centre of Excellence (CoE) is where knowledge and learning around key HR processes is formulated and then disseminated to the HR function and through the HRBPs to the business. It is here that the deep technical expertise within the function would typically reside, with a focus on design rather than implementation. The policies implemented by the Shared Service Centre will also be created here. The Centre of Expertise provides a more efficient method of focusing specialist expertise and leveraging it across the business. Typical examples of CoE would include subject matter experts who set the policies and principles that govern Employee Relations, Learning and Development, Talent Management and Reward practices with in an organization.

The type of expertise required in these central roles will be heavily influenced by the type of organization supported. For example, although the generic categories of reward, learning and employee relations are likely to be found in most companies – reward and performance management may form a larger part of the focus in the HR department of a law firm whilst employee relations would need to be a core capability in a unionized manufacturing company where day to day engagement with union representative may take up a significant part of an HR professional's day.

The CoEs also have a key role to play as environmental scanners – ensuring an appropriate awareness of market best practice in individual functional areas. Identifying how the latest developments in HR strategy might be applied to an organization's commercial or competitive advantage is an important part of this role. However, slavish application of the latest HR fad or 'ivory tower' thinking needs to be avoided. The governance role of the HR leadership team can help ensure that the correct balance is maintained.

SHARED SERVICES

Far from the common perception that shared services is the administrative backwater of the HR function, they should more accurately be described as the delivery engine. As more organizations move towards a shared service model to deliver the administrative and advisory elements of the HR function, the shared service centre is where the majority of both the HR headcount and the HR cost base will lie.

Shared services will channel day-to-day employee and line manager contact through the most appropriate route for resolution, focusing on getting that enquiry or transaction completed in the most efficient way.

Getting the SSC right is also fundamental in supporting the CoE and the success of the HRBP model. By creating this first point of contact as a filter for basic queries, only those issues that require a higher level of expert intervention will be raised to the CoE staff or escalated to HRBPs if necessary.

CHANNEL MANAGEMENT AND SERVICE TIERING

We have already talked about the importance of managing the contact channels into HR. An effective shared services operation will take this one step further and have a very clear approach to tiering activity. The scope of activity covered by a shared services operation will vary by organization, but at its most sophisticated may cover services across the full employee life cycle. The successful handling of these processes will then be organized across a number of roles, offering a variety of tiers of access, (typically Tier 0 through to Tier 3, see Figure 4.2).

TIER 0 – SELF SERVICE

Tier 0 is aimed at generating economies of scale from the delivery of both everyday HR information and the processing of basic HR transactions . Self-service access creates efficiencies for managers and employees as well as HR staff. This self-service layer of the shared services operation may be largely passive – in that it is just the provision of on line information via

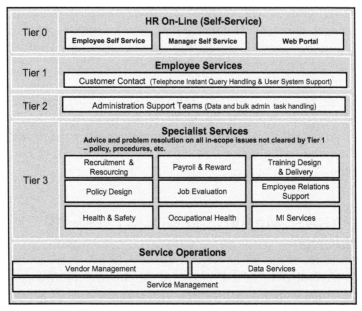

Figure 4.2   Tiering of service within the SSC. Orion Partners 2008

a company intranet, allowing staff to view policy information but not to actually undertake any transactions for themselves. Employee and Manager Self-Service technology allows certain services to be delivered on-line, enabling managers and employees to access their data, information and undertake basic transactions directly at a time of their choosing. It also acts as a repository for policy documentation and guidance.

As the entry point into self service, HR portals can also include functionality to support other activity, such as the recruitment process where newly appointed employees complete joining and induction documentation online prior to starting work.

Ideally any portal access will be integrated to other areas of support activity – that is, finance, procurement, knowledge management. With many of the major enterprise technology solutions (ERPs) provided by software houses such as SAP and Oracle, the linkages between these areas are automated. For example, the information contained in the HR section of the system on roles and the organization's hierarchy can be used to drive authorizations in the procurement process. Without technology of this kind, functionality of this kind can be complex to achieve, requiring a single 'sign-on' to what can be multiple pieces of technology that are not necessarily integrated.

However, if line managers and employees can access the HR service as part of the way they go about their day-to-day business, there is a much greater chance that they will use e-HR technology. This is a useful principle for every element of the service's design.

From an efficiency perspective, encouraging employees to use self service is likely to have clear advantages. The service can be available 24/7 with no associated costs in HR headcount. Encouraging increased usage of self service will typically be at the heart of the performance improvement strategy of any shared services operation.

On the other hand, designing a solution that is overly reliant on self service in the early stages of a move to this model can be a high risk. Levels of IT literacy or indeed just the practical issues of access to hardware and network capacity may well be limiting factors. We have seen a number of examples of self service applications that are operating on a network infrastructure that quickly begin to creak under the the volume of transactions generated by self service. If the service promise has been 'quick and easy access to HR' and the reality is a frozen screen when an employee tries to input a holiday request, the reputation of the new HR model will tarnish very easily.

The number of employees who access on-line services needs to be considered in the context of the jobs people do and the environment in which they operate A large utilities company took the decision for all field-based engineering staff to record their overtime through self service accessed via kiosk facilities in regional offices. Fridays saw long queues of maintenance vans outside regional offices as engineering staff waited to log on to input their claims. The result clearly increased the efficiency of the HR administration department but had directly the opposite effect on the productivity of the company's core business.

Typical questions and transactions processed effectively via self-service include those summarized in Table 4.1.

Table 4.1   Typical Tier self-service transactions

Typical transactions and activities that will be performed via self-service	
Employees	**Line Managers**
Update personal details	Access online policies, step by step guides and
Search for and book training	how to instructions for all people management policies
Request annual leave	Access template letters, forms and documents for
Search and view HR policies	all people management policies and activities
View employment package (terms and conditions)	Track and monitor absence (update team time and attendance records)
Update competences/skill profiles	Approve employee self service requests
	Delegate/redirect authority to local administrator

Table 4.1 *Concluded*

Search and apply for internal vacancies	Record employee absence
View payslip details	Enter vacancy information to commence recruitment process
Submit expenses	Receive and view job applicant details in preparation for interviews
Submit overtime claims	
Apply for season ticket	Manage new starter administration
View training course materials	Managing training and development (approval of courses)
Withdraw from training courses	Complete performance review of team
View HR FAQs	Employee modeling/ budgeting (manpower planning and reports)
Access to eForms	Analyse team trends and costs (reports)
View online policy guidelines, access template forms, letters and how to guides	Override shift patterns

TIER 1 – FRONTLINE SUPPORT

Tier 1 support involves providing skilled HR generalist support for managers and employees where they have been unable to find the answer they require on the web portal. Contact is typically via phone though can also be provided electronically. It is advisable to ensure that this is based around purpose built eForms, (rather than free form emails which may result in more contact and therefore more activity) or via automated workflow that is directly built into the HR technology. Service agents in this part of the shared service operation should have access to systems and information at a sufficient level of detail to answer the majority of standard HR queries. Queries that require more in-depth technical expertise such as a complex disciplinary problem or grievance would be transferred to a specialist or case worker (Tier 3.) The service and organization design for this element of the service should enable the requirements of four out five contacts to be concluded straight away. Often referred to as 'one and done', a target first contact clearance of +80 per cent is a good benchmark standard, although initially clearance rates of 30–40 per cent may be experienced, achieving the target benchmark within six to twelve months of launching a new service.

Typical questions and transactions processed via self-service and first level SSC agents include those outlined in the Table 4.2.

Table 4.2   Typical Tier 1 transactions

Typical questions and transactions raised by:	
Employees	**Line Managers**
HR policy and staff handbook queries and advice (incl 'where can I find etc, 1st line HR systems support)	HR policy and staff handbook queries and advice (where can I find, what do I do?);
Checking and updating personal data	Checking and updating personal data;
Entitlements (policies and process)	Changing or authorising personal data for employees;
L&D – information, enrolments, cancellations, induction, course evaluation	Authorising HR transactions (for example, staff leave requests, training etc);
Resourcing – vacancy/application	Request reports;
Information, applications (alternative formats – paper, Braille)	Resourcing – raise vacancies etc;
Performance Mgt – status, copies	Performance management – completing;
	Leave and absence – recording absence, approve leave

Table 4.2 *Concluded*

Typical questions and transactions raised by:	
Reward – queries, entitlements, child care voucher requests, pay queries, Travel and Subsistence Leave and absence – queries and entitlements, notification and processes Leaving queries, entitlements, notification Grievance and Disciplinary queries, process and notification Pay cycle queries and issues	Reward queries, entitlements, authorize changes, request MI; Leaving queries, entitlements, notification, Last Day of Work (LDoW); Grievance and Disciplinary – queries, process and notification; Pay cycle administration queries

TIER 2 – TRANSACTION PROCESSING

Tier 2 is the transactional heart of the SSC, where high volume administrative activity is undertaken. This team will handle large-scale data management and bulk administration tasks (supporting, for example: recruitment campaign administration; updating of organizational structures in the HR system; bulk admin tasks around annual appraisals; and year end payroll related administration). Work can arrive here directly via a number of channels – via self service directly from line managers or employees, via automated workflow from Tier 1 service agents. This will mean service agents posting work requests into virtual work stacks/queues from which team members will take activity. It can also arrive via the more traditional routes of post or fax. Where volume warrants the investment, scanning and electronic document management technology can be used to transform the paper trails into electronic data that streamlines still further the administration process.

This team will not have direct contact with line managers and employees as all calls will be handled by the service agents in Tier 1 or escalated to specialists in Tier 3. However, it is common practice to train individuals in these teams in generalist HR support and customer service skills so that in times of peak demand they are able to transfer to Tier 1 activities and handle incoming calls and workflow requests as part of the front-desk operation. It enables the SSC to respond in a cost effective manner to variations in demand for Tier 1 services. This capability takes time to develop and needs to be built into the operational training plan.

TIER 3 – CASE WORK AND SPECIALIST SERVICES

Tier 3 is where the specialist HR skills will be concentrated in the SSC. Roles will vary according to the scope of shared services delivery, but may include specialist case workers who will support employee relations activity through to recruitment and learning specialists. Whereas the majority of staff in Tiers 1 and 2 will be based physically in one central shared services location, it often the case that staff in this part of the shared services operation may be field based so that they can be deployed to support activity that requires face to face contact.

Tier 3 marks the point of service overlaps with the HR Business Partners and Centres of Excellence. If specialists in Tier 3 are unable to answer or respond appropriately to the query, they may involve an HRBP or CoE team member who is able to offer more detailed advice and/or may be the point of escalation for a decision on the appropriate course of action to be taken. The SSC specialist will be responsible for keeping in contact with the HRBP or CoE to track the case's progress and to update the case management system.

The SSC Specialists should be trained and supported by sufficient technology and data access to provide advice and problem solving on issues related to complex and sensitive policy interpretation and procedural issues across a range of the whole spectrum of HR processes, including:

- Resource Management – recruitment, transfers, secondments and workforce planning.

- Learning and Development – talent management, training needs analysis, competencies and evaluation activities.

- Pay/Reward – reward and remuneration, job evaluation, payroll, attendance, and exit management.

- Employee Relations – grievance and disciplinary cases, capability (ill health and performance) cases.

- Industrial relations – leading and advising on Union consultations and negotiations.

- Performance Management – appraisal review, objectives, 360° assessment.

- Compensation and Benefits – benchmarking, entitlements.

- Advising line management with options to address a wide range of complex policy and procedural issues.

- Working on, and subsequently closing, complex cases opened by the Tier 1 team.

- Advising Managers when HR decisions might need to be taken outside of defined policy and process.

- Integrating HR process best practice and techniques to enhance the overall HR delivery capability.

- Working with CoEs to design fit-for-purpose HR policies.

- Working with the SSC Service Management team and other colleagues to deliver an integrated HR service compliant with agreed performance levels.

The technology used to support the service in this area may include case management tools as well as specialist recruitment, learning or performance management applications. These may form part of an integrated suite of tools within an enterprise solution such as SAP or Oracle, or may be 'tools on top' which are separate specialist applications that are ideally linked by an electronic interface to the primary HR database where master employee data is held.

Typical questions and transactions supported by Tier 3 SSC Specialists are shown in Table 4.3.

The team should be organized so that:

- Their deep functional HR process and policy knowledge can be accessed by all staff regardless of their grade or location.

- Complex cases can be prioritized and tracked using a case management system.

- They are available to support customers face-to-face if required.

- They act as the single point of contact between the customer and the SSC for HR queries and requests that need to be resolved over an extended period of time (that is, those more complex queries which cannot be resolved within Tier 1).

In addition, a core element of the Tier 3 team's roles will be providing project resource and expertise to both HRBP

Table 4.3   Typical Tier 3 transactions

Typical questions and transactions raised by:	
Employees	**Line Managers**
Learning and Development – Detailed HR policy and process advice, specific course attendance activities Resourcing – Detailed HR policy and process advice, specific advice on application process Pay and Reward – Specific detailed issues/ queries Employee/Industrial Relations – complex and/or serious issues that require specialist knowledge and guidance	Learning and Development – Detailed policy and process advice, specific course attendance activities, setting up specific courses and managing all course logistics Resourcing – Setting-up a recruitment campaign and placing adverts, tracking vacancies, liaison with 3rd parties as needed Pay – reward detailed policy, guidance and procedures Employee relations/ performance management queries regarding a complex case or issue

initiatives and CoE strategy and policy development activity. The interaction, relationship and detailed activities, defining the boundaries between Tier 3 and the CoE or HRBPs must be clearly defined. This becomes particularly pertinent where more specialist HR activities are dealt with, such as the hand-off of a complex disciplinary case to an HRBP. As a principle, multiple hand-offs are to be avoided; therefore it is important that the nature of work and how it will be handled *between* Tiers 1, 3 and the HRBP is clearly defined.

In our experience, the way information about cases and levels of activity is shared between theses teams will often dictate how well the system works across tiers. We have worked with a number of our clients who have included case worker support within the scope of their SSC, to develop ways of working that encourage proactive sharing of information through specific policy forums as well as case-conference type arrangements to involve BPs or CoE specialists in more complex cases. It is also typical to find that the early levels of nervousness that may be experienced by HR generalists handing over case activity to specialist teams begin to disappear once the service has time to establish itself.

The four levels tiers of service are summarized in Figure 4.3.

SUPPORTING HR SHARED SERVICES

We have used the phrase 'delivery engine' to describe the shared services operation. Another description, which we use prejudice, is the 'HR factory'. In the same way as a well run manufacturing unit relies on the disciplines of production planning and maintenance, an effective shared services operation needs to have the right level of operational

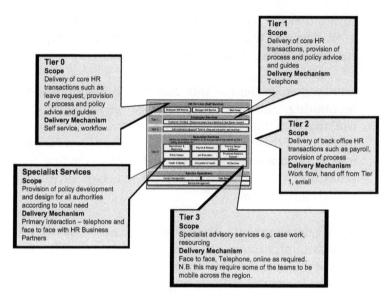

Figure 4.3   Service tiering summary – scope and delivery mechanisms. Orion Partners 2008

management support as well as the right support tools to run smoothly. This is an area in which many HR functions fail to invest; an unfortunate decision as it can be what makes the difference between the basic delivery of standardized administrative service and an effective service operation.

We refer to this part of the SSC as the Service Operations function, whose role it is to provide the governance and management framework of the SSC. The Service Operations function is typically comprised of six key service areas:

1. Account management – this team manages the relationship between the shared service and the business units. It is their role to report on service performance and manage any customer satisfaction issues. It is also their role to

ensure that the SSC is kept up to date with any changes in the business that are likely to affect either the types or volume of services required from the SSC.

2. Service management – this function is responsible for monitoring and measuring service performance and working with the service delivery teams to identify the root cause if there are any issues. They also play a valuable role in planning the capacity of the SSC, ensuring that peaks and troughs in demand are managed across the various service tiers.

3. Service development – This team is focused on service and process improvement. Although a culture of continuous improvement is desirable across the HRSSC, we have found it to be beneficial to have a specialist resource that can dedicate time and effort to the improvement of existing services, or the introduction or transfer in of new services. It is in this part of the operation that you may build in specific expertise in performance improvement techniques such as Six Sigma.

4. Vendor management – Vendor management is particularly important if benefits from improved shared HR procurement are to be realized. These can often represent a significant component of HR expenditure and improvement in both cost and quality in the management of third party delivery may well be a critical component of any financial case for change. These are not typically skills to be found within HR functions, and it may be that they will be drawn from other areas within the organization.

5. Data services – specialist teams in systems administration and data services, whose role it is to maintain the systems required to run the service.

6. Finance management – The requirement for dedicated finance management support will vary depending on the size and complexity of the shared services operation. It may just be about basic budget management, but if cross charging for services becomes more sophisticated, with the introduction of transactional charging for example, a higher level of finance resource will be needed.

A comprehensive shared services solution (see Figure 4.4) will also benefit from best practice use of the underlying technology and decision support tools such as:

● Contact Management System (CMS) – a workflow system to generate and manage work requests as a result of a call or eForm. These systems are also known as Customer Relationship Management (CRM) systems.

● Digital document management.

● Knowledge management systems (covering policy and procedures) and frequently asked question databases.

● The CMS solution will integrate the document imaging, self-service, email and telephone calls received by the SSC, providing a single comprehensive view of the customer throughout their time as an employee.

Increasingly HR shared services also form part of wider enterprise shared services operations covering Finance, Procurement and IT activity. Sharing the investment in the supporting infrastructure and adopting the principles of work management outlined below will drive even greater efficiency.

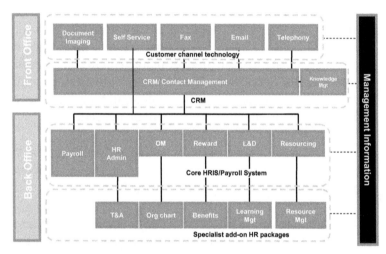

Figure 4.4   Typical HRSSC technology architecture

BASIC PRINCIPLES OF WORK MANAGEMENT WITHIN SSC

The basic principles of managing the internal workload for an SSC are:

- The majority of queries will be resolved at the first point of contact at the web portal.

- There should be clearly defined referral routes for queries and processing transactions.

- Clearly defined processes, scripting, FAQs and checklists are required for all the major transactions and customer queries.

- SSC management are responsible for ensuring that performance metrics are achieved and surpassed.

- Transactions will be 'time-bound', that is, if a transaction is not handled within a set time period, it is escalated (initially to a Tier 1 team leader) for action.

- The organsiation and the systems include the flexibility to allocate skilled resource to peaks in workload.

- Workflow will be used to direct tasks to the appropriate skilled resource.

(5) Adapting the Model

In Chapter 4, we provided a review of each of the constituent parts of the HR delivery model. However, as we identified at the start of the book, although there will be similarities between the form and function of each part of the model across different organizations, what is critical is applying them in context and ensuring that the fit is right for the business you are in. Determining the precise scope of each part of the delivery model will be a process that is influenced by a number of factors (see Figure 5.1):

- Size and scale of the organization – a shared service model for delivery can only be truly effective when economies of scale can be achieved, justifying the required investment in process standardization and e-enablement.

- Geographical complexity – some services will always require local knowledge and may also need face to face support. In a business with wide national or international spread this will tend to lead to a regional dimension for some elements of service provision.

- Business unit autonomy vs. central control – the power dimension within the organization will also influence how the service is structured. If the powerbase of the organization is with a strong corporate centre and there is limited scope for individual business units to influence local strategy, this will lead more naturally to a wider scope for shared services provision. The level of homogeneity between business units and their respective workforces will also influence the shape of the service that is right for an organization.

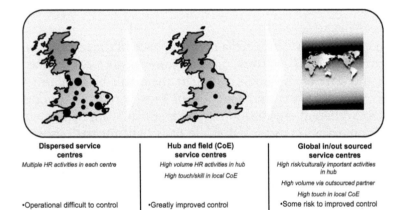

Dispersed service centres *Multiple HR activities in each centre*	**Hub and field (CoE) service centres** *High volume HR activities in hub* *High touch/skill in local CoE*	**Global in/out sourced service centres** *High risk/culturally important activities in hub* *High volume via outsourced partner* *High touch in local CoE*
•Operational difficult to control	•Greatly improved control	•Some risk to improved control
•Limited 'shared' infrastructure	•Improved 'shared' infrastructure	•Maximised 'shared' infrastructure
•Close BU support	•Close BU support	•Some risk to close BU support
•Limited economies of scale and skill	•Improved economies of scale and skill	•Maximised economies of scale and skill

Figure 5.1   Service centre distribution – implications for service delivery

BREADTH AND DEPTH OF SCOPE

Many organizations are fully supportive of the centralization of transactional activity in the traditional areas of HR administration and payroll. Although this is seen as business critical activity, it is non-contentious when considering centralization. As long as these processes are delivered in a timely and accurate fashion, organizations are broadly comfortable that they be delivered from a unit that may be geographically remote from the business units they support. This is because these processes are discrete and require minimal handoffs with the business.

This is not the case for more embedded processes such as recruitment, performance management or employee relations and it is here where there is likely to be much more extensive debate about where activity should sit and where accountability should lie.

The broader the scope of the activity considered for shared services delivery, and the deeper the level of expertise that can be consolidated into the model, the greater impact on the service delivered – both from an efficiency and effectiveness perspective. Economies of scale in administration will drive improvements in the transactional areas. Economies of skill in specialist areas such as caseworking or recruitment will drive higher levels of consistency. More effective methods of sharing knowledge and best practice, as well as greater visibility of the trends will in turn shape the development of the HR strategy.

'MAKE OR BUY?' IN-HOUSE BUILD OR OUTSOURCED DELIVERY?

Debates about the scope of service and decisions about which activities should sit where will be come even more intense when an organization considers outsourcing parts of the service delivery model. Some HR activities have been routinely outsourced for many years- payroll and outplacement for example. With the growth of business process outsourcing, full scale HR Outsourcing (HRO) is a real possibility and will form a fundamental part of the decision making process that needs to be considered during the initial service design. For some organizations, keeping all aspects of the function in-house and under direct control is the only route for consideration. If outsourcing is an option, this will be driven by a number of factors including:

- The stability of current operations – many quote the old adage ' never outsource a mess' and see the need to ensure that processes are stable and activity is under control before considering outsourcing

- The company/organization's history of outsourcing – it is unlikely that the HR function will volunteer to be the guinea pigs for business process outsourcing. Areas where the outsourced solution has a longer track record and is more commoditized in nature such as desk top support for IT would be more likely to be the first to adopt the model

- The culture and politics- it may just be culturally or politically unacceptable for an organization to consider outsourcing. This is particularly the case now that the larger outsourcing providers are using an offshore model to reduce their cost of operation. This is likely to be a more sensitive issue in some organizations than others, particularly in the public sector where the notion of offshoring activity will have more complex political implications.

For others, a more pragmatic approach is taken to maximize the economies of scale.

Partnering with a service supplier can bring capital cost benefits, particularly around IT spend which can still account for up to 80 per cent of an in-house HR solution's transformation budget. The supplier's existing relationships with other third party vendors for example, recruitment or training providers can be leveraged and the SSC technology and service is already in place. How much outsourcing costs depends on the type of solution put in place and how it is serviced. For example, a single country solution with a near shore (in the same country or region as the business) shared service centre will have a different cost base to a multi-country solution that involves a mix of near and far-shore (such as India or China) locations with twenty four hour service, 365 days a year. Outsourcing is not for every organization, but it is becoming an acceptable solution for an increasing number for part or all of their back-office processes.

INTEGRATING THE MODEL

Whatever the final decision on scope and structure – what is important is clarity. It should be clear where activities and accountabilities sit so that the function can organise itself to realize maximum value. However, all too often, this is where the design process is left incomplete. Significant time is spent in identifying what each service area will do and how they will operate, but minimal time is spent on establishing how the different parts of the function will integrate and work together. The result can often be an HR service that is fragmented and disconnected in the eyes of the customer.

Integration, and the allocation of roles and responsibilities this facilitates, is critical and must operate at a number of levels (see Figure 5.2):

• Operationally: through common processes and data.

• Intellectually: through effective sharing of knowledge.

- Socially: through a common sense of 'one HR' identity.

- Emotionally: through shared values and sense of purpose.

Operational integration- is about ensuring that, where ever possible, there is 'one best way' that uses information derived from one common data source. Although there will be legitimate reasons for different policies and procedures, common processes and common definitions about the way in which data is used, even if it not stored in the same systems, are critical to ensuing an integrated approach. Some organizations shy away from the concept of shared services on the basis that they have a multitude of different terms and conditions of employment and believe that shared services will mean a mass harmonization programme that is not achievable. This is not the case. As long as organizations can work to standardise the way service is delivered – in other words, how a query is answered, how managers access information – then the fact that policies and procedures themselves may be different is just something that needs to be factored into the way the way knowledge is shared.

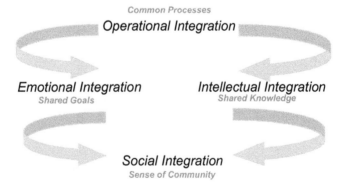

Figure 5.2   Levels of integration. Orion Partners 2006

Intellectual Integration – effective knowledge sharing across the HR function is one of the ways of ensuring that there is clarity on roles and responsibilities and also that different parts of the function are able to adapt when there are changes that affect some or all parts of the service. It is also a means of building skills to ensure that individuals are able to build careers by moving across the function.

Social Integration – this is nothing more complicated than ensuring there is a sense of community across the function by encouraging interactions between different teams. This can be through formal networking opportunities or buddying and mentoring schemes, but also just as simple as providing people with the opportunity to get together at social events.

Emotional Integration – people will feel a greater sense of commitment to something when they believe there is a common purpose. In formal terms it can be helpful to drive some of these behaviours through team or individual performance objectives that target the mutual success of different parts of the function. Borrowing techniques from marketing colleagues, a common brand used to link different parts of the HR service can also be a powerful way of ensuring people feel linked in to a common HR agenda. This also has the additional benefits of providing a cohesive image to the customer; an advantage not to be ignored.

⑥ New HR – New Line Management?

We have already highlighted that a new way of working for HR will only succeed with support from the business. Using a definition of the service based firmly on business needs is the key to ensuring that the service delivery model will work. We have described in detail the implications for a new way of delivering service on the role of HR and the way it is structured. Changes in the HR delivery model will also have knock-on implications for the role of the line manager and the way they manage their people.

Changes to the delivery model will not typically change line managers' accountabilities for people, but they will change the way in which these responsibilities are executed. With HR services that are easier to access and self service tools that are user-friendly and intuitive, managers could and should be responsible for a wide range of the processes needed to manage their staff. (see Figure 6.1)

For skilled line managers, experienced in managing people effectively, this will not be an issue. For newer managers or those with development needs in this area, it is the role of the

	Assumptions: Supervising a front line team, limited span of control **First Line**	**Assumptions:** operational manager maybe managing a large part of a service **Middle Mgr**	**Assumptions:** a head of service, strategic manager **Senior Mgr**
Key Processes	All day to day people management processes – e.g. attendance management, performance management	All day to day for own team Planning and budgeting, target and KPI management	As middle, also setting and reviewing targets and KPIs, service standards etc. Identifying strategic objectives. Accountable for all delivery of process at lower levels
People management skills	Decision making, performance management, managing to targets, rapport, recruitment and selection, customer service, systems	As first, also networking, analytical, influencing, relationship management, business awareness, commercial understanding, resource management	As middle, also negotiation, relationship management and influencing at senior level. External networking as well as internal.
Underpinning beliefs and behaviours	I own my own team, I am manager of people. People management is core part of role, e.g. seeing value in carrying out people management processes, not as distraction from 'real' job	As first, also 'let go and lead', focus on own direct reports, not their reports too. Manage by risk and exception, forward planning and outcomes not process focused. Innovate, drive continuous improvement	As middle, focus on identifying opportunities and stretching team. Develop high level overall organisational view and external

Figure 6.1   Typical line management accountability

HR function to provide learning and development paths to that will equip them with the skills they need.

The way in which these changes are communicated and sold in is critical as it can be easy for managers to perceive them as an increasing burden rather than empowering them to take responsibility for the management of their people. Success relies heavily on user-friendly self-service tools which make the basics quick and easy to do and on a supportive and responsive HR service that is flexible enough to provide the level of support as required. These factors are important when sizing the HR operation – a task that will be analysed in more detail in the next chapter.

In designing the organization, it is important to size the level of resource against the support line managers need across the typical range of HR activities: what can managers realistically be expected to do with the skills and tools they have at their disposal? Expecting to deliver a 'light touch' service with limited face-to-face support in cases where the level of manager capability is low is a recipe for problems.

Understanding these skills gaps when planning the implementation of the new service is important as it will drive the focus of the change management support required. An impact assessment that identifies the key changes should be used to underpin the planning of training and communications.

In Figure 6.2, we have provided an example of a summary impact assessment. The assessment describes what the impact will be of key changes in the HR delivery model. The different impacts will have different implications for the kinds of activity required to help manage the change. For example, if there were fundamental changes to line managers' roles and

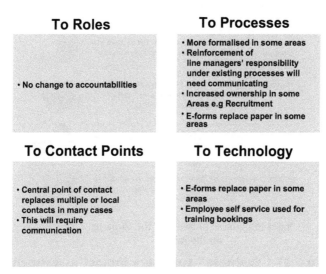

To Roles

• No change to accountabilities

To Processes

• More formalised in some areas
• Reinforcement of
  line managers' responsibility
  under existing processes will
  need communicating
• Increased ownership in some
  Areas e.g Recruitment
• E-forms replace paper in some
  areas

To Contact Points

• Central point of contact
  replaces multiple or local
  contacts in many cases
• This will require
  communication

To Technology

• E-forms replace paper in some
  areas
• Employee self service used for
  training bookings

Figure 6.2   Example – Change impact summary

accountabilities, this may have a significant impact. It might mean training managers, but in some organizations where role descriptions are highly prescriptive, it may even mean a requirement to negotiate or compensate managers for changes to their roles. In our experience, this is rarely the case but it has definitely been an initial negotiating stance which has been adopted by some trade unions resistant to the proposed changes.

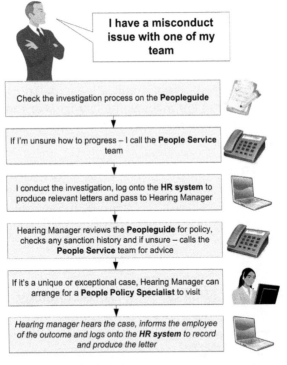

'I get the advice I need and the tools to do the job'

Figure 6.3   Example – summary impact assessment

Line managers also have a role to play as change agents. HR can instigate, facilitate and own the coordination of people issues in change programmes, but it is the line manager that delivers and owns the overall outcome. Similarly, line managers have the closest relationship with their people and understand the issues and challenges they face and what motivates them. The illustration in Figure 6.4 shows how changes to the service will impact a line manager's role. It is these kinds of communication tools that can be very helpful in ensuring line managers are also able to sell and support the changes with their people.

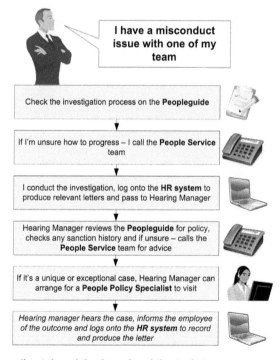

'I get the advice I need and the tools to do the job'

Figure 6.4   Example – what the service means

 # Sizing the Operation and Building the Business Case

We started this book by examining some of the underlying driving forces for HR transformation. Unsurprisingly, one of the key areas of focus was cost. A need to deliver more for less is often at the heart of the move to look at new ways of providing service. However, we have also sought to ensure the appropriate balance of emphasis is given to the cost agenda– as we have witnessed too many programmes for change that have been focused purely on the need to make cost savings. They have resulted in short term cost reduction made through relatively arbitrary cuts in expenditure. Delivery of a lower cost service is only achieved by fundamentally reviewing the way service is delivered and re-engineering large components to ensure that the model is sustainable.

We have placed a very deliberate emphasis on the concept of service, as we believe that this is what lies at the heart of effective design. However, the design still needs to be developed within the context of what the organization can afford and this chapter focuses on sizing the service and building the business case for change.

UNDERSTANDING YOUR COSTS

In simplistic terms the business case for change (see Figure 7.1) relies on understanding the following three major cost components:

- The cost of service delivery under the current model.

- The forecast cost of service delivery under the future model.

- The cost of implementation – for example, technology, facilities, programme management, selection, assessment, development and any severance costs.

These represent the direct costs associated with people, technology, infrastructure and third party expenditure. However, it is likely that there will be significant amounts of indirect expenditure that should also be assessed as part of the business case. This involves measuring the impact of inefficient HR delivery on the productivity of line managers and employees. For example, the savings that could be achieved through simpler and more efficient ways of managing employee absence may actually generate much higher savings in the long term than any initial cost reduction within the HR function itself.

Identifying these individual benefit streams, ensuring an accurate baseline of current cost and establishing the appropriate mechanisms are in place to track the targeted reductions are core disciplines in any transformation programme.

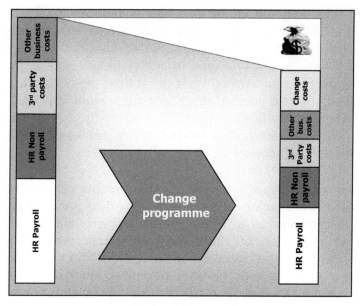

Figure 7.1   Components of the business case

SIZING THE OPERATION

Establishing a clear and accurate picture of the costs of current service delivery can be problematic. However the greater challenge can be in determining the accurate sizing of the new model to establish a realistic estimate of the future cost base. The theory is very simple and there are two key dimensions to understand:

1. Current cost base – what does your HR service cost?

2. Current activity profile – what do you deliver? In other words, how many individuals do you hire? How many pay transactions do your process? How many days of training do you deliver?

An understanding of the cost base is generally achievable but establishing a clear picture of the service volumes that drive these costs can be more difficult. In many organizations, HR activity is not measured in any systematic way and so the ability to understand what lies behind the costs can be difficult. At this point, if this information is not available, it will be a worthwhile investment to generate the data for your core HR processes through sample activity analysis as it will be critical to the accurate sizing of the new model.

Having understood the costs of current service delivery and established a picture of the volumes required, the next task is to compare the 'as is' and 'to be' processes and identify what proportion of effort and cost will be removed by standardization, automation or elimination. This may sound like a daunting task, however remember, the data is only required for the core processes that are either high volume or high impact – typically those for which a service specification has been developed as described in Chapter 3. It is not necessary to undertake this assessment for every individual HR process, but for those that drive the bulk of HR activity.

BENCHMARKING – A RULE OF THUMB

It is at this point that external benchmark data can be extremely useful in helping sense check estimates of what level of resource will be required. There are significant amounts of industry specific data now available which will help give an indication of what levels of performance can be expected. The table shown below (Table 7.1) is typical of the kind of data available and can provide a relative point of comparison that is very useful. But beware, slavish application of industry ratios needs to be avoided as the inability to ensure a like for like comparison will always mean that the specific requirements of each organization will have a role to play in determining precise numbers.

If feasible, we always encourage organizations to err on the side of caution and be conservative in the level of efficiency they expect to achieve in the early days of the implementation of a new model. Not everything will work smoothly at the outset but the business is unlikely to be forgiving of any perceived dip in service delivery. Organizations only really have one opportunity to get it right and allowing some flexibility in the model in the early days, in order to avoid a perceived risk of failure is very important.

Table 7.1   Example ratios for 'sizing' a shared services operation based on Orion Partners client engagements 2002–2008

Tier 1 Employee query and contact support rations	1:1250 (In-house operation aiming for 80% first point call resolution) 1:2000 HR BPO provider serving multiple clients
Tier 2 Fulfillment	1:2000 (including HR, payroll, recruitment and training admin)
Tier 3 Payroll	1:3000
Tier 3 Resourcing	1:130 vacancies
Tier 3 Training	1:180 days effective annual trainer utilization
Tier 3 Employee Relations	1:90–100 cases per annum

THE COST OF CHANGE

The final 'element we referred to in the introduction to this chapter was the cost of delivering the change itself. There are a number of variables that will affect the cost of implementation:

- The level of technology investment required – in our experience, this may represent up to 80 per cent of the change budget. It is unlikely that the same percentage of the benefits will be realized as a result of technology, but it is important to recognize how this investment can be used to best effect.

- The use of in-house vs external resource – organizations will vary in the level of in-house capability they have to manage a programme of this kind. Many resort to using external programme management support which can often be very beneficial. However it is important that any reliance on external resource to support the change does not lead to a lack of internal ownership as it will be this that will ensure that the change is embedded and the new ways of working achieve what they set out to achieve.

- Incremental vs big bang – the approach to implementation may vary according to many different factors. There is an element of the way in which organsiations approach the implementation of large scale change that is driven by their culture. Some may feel the need to develop a proof of concept that is then piloted extensively before implementation whilst others may be less risk adverse (or foolhardy) and drive through change in a more aggressive fashion. Scale and complexity will also be significant factors as will the level of technological change involved.

All these elements will affect the profile of the change programme in terms of time, work effort and cost. A shorter implementation timeline may require higher levels of resource and cost but with earlier payback and realization of benefits.

- Skillset match – We have already identified that it is likely that the new model will require a different skills mix. This may mean that in addition to any costs associated with individuals leaving the organization, costs will also be incurred in recruiting new capabilities or developing these in-house through targeted training interventions. It is also likely that during the implementation an excess of resource will be required to manage the transition from one model to the next, both to smooth the transition from one to the other, but also to ensure that 'business as usual' service is delivered during the implementation period.

TOUGH CHOICES

The investment criteria for any major programme will almost certainly be centrally predetermined with a target payback period and standard return on investment percentages (ROI) and net present value calculations (NPV). These calculations are used to help businesses make tough objective decisions about the way in which they prioritise their investment. Unless the HR function is extremely inefficient, it will often be a challenge to meet these targets based on pure cost reduction within the function. It is for this reason that HR must be able to articulate and quantify in business terms the value that will be created through a more effective HR service. Numbers talk and they will need to be compelling for the finance function to listen.

⑧ Managing the Service

The revised structure of HR brings all the benefits of being able to supply agreed levels of standardised services and processes to the business. Once the operating model is running at its optimum level of performance, this standardised approach will build the organization's respect for the function. The improved management information will also enable a meaningful dialogue between HRBPs and the senior management of the business area for which they are responsible. The value-add activity can then start to become part of the normal business planning process.

The HRBP is now equipped to anticipate people management challenges facing the business before they become major problems and work with the business, and where appropriate with specialist resources from the CoE, to plan an avoidance strategy. The HRBP will also be in a position to incorporate people into the business' medium and long-term planning process and help define the scope of appropriate human resource strategies to support broader organizational objectives. The HR Leadership team will be well placed to drive the corporate HR strategy and ensure that best practice HR policy, strategy and activities are being implemented to meet the delivery capability of the function and the needs of the business.

GOVERNANCE STRUCTURE

As with any business function, the HR operating model is required to operate within a clearly defined governance framework to ensure that it continues to supply services in line with customer requirements.

There are a number of key assumptions underpinning the model. These are that there are:

- Clear lines of responsibility and authority between each level of governance.

- Clearly defined lines of responsibility and accountability between HR and its customers.

- Clearly defined lines of responsibility between each area of HR.

These assumptions should ensure that the most influential groups cannot exert undue influence on all or some of the services offered by HR. All parts of the HR team need to be represented and involved in the governance arrangements so members of the HRBP, HRSSC and CoE teams will each be part of the governance structure.

The governance framework describes these proposed arrangements as illustrated in Figure 8.1. These responsibilities will typically be delivered through a number of different bodies and meetings.

The purposes, membership and role of these boards are described in the remainder of this section.

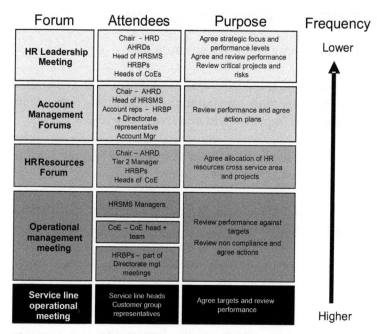

Figure 8.1   Illustrative HR governance framework

HR LEADERSHIP MEETING

This forum is responsible for taking an overall picture of all the activities within the HR function, setting overall direction, reviewing performance against agreed targets and managing key projects and risks. At this forum the overall strategic business direction will be discussed and HR activity agreed.

ACCOUNT MANAGEMENT/CUSTOMER MANAGERS' FORUM

This forum is responsible for ensuring that:

- The overall shared service is aligned with customer expectations and operational assumptions, especially continuous improvement and cost effectiveness targets.

- HR shared services can hear at first hand and respond to direct customer feedback.

- HR shared services can flex service delivery to adapt to ongoing business need.

- Performance against a jointly agreed Service Level Agreement is measured.

- The businesses understand the operational dynamics of shared services. (for example, changes to scope, capacity planning issues)

In short, to ensure a focused two-way dialogue is maintained between the HR service provider and customers.

The forum should focus on:

- Service performance:

    - Often against formal service level agreements;
    - Transaction volumes;
    - Issues, resolutions, effectiveness of actions taken;
    - Reviewing customer feedback.

- Future plans:

  - Upcoming activity;
  - Change requests.

- Service Improvement:

  - Reviewing recommendations on improvements to service (and monitoring progress of follow-up actions);
  - Scope and extensions to service;
  - Mid/long term capacity planning.

HR RESOURCES FORUM

Given that HR resources will be utilised jointly by shared services, HRBPs and CoEs, and all areas of HR will be required to work jointly on various projects, a regular forum will be required to review the allocation of resource according to workload and project need.

At this forum, the current resource allocation will be reviewed. Requests for resource from HRBPs and CoEs will be evaluated along with the upcoming operational needs of the HRSSC. Resource decisions are made with the operational needs of the organization and the development needs of the individuals within HR in mind. Effective deployment and utilization of resource will be a key part the career development and talent management of HR staff. The chair of the resource forum will be expected to review the cost of resource deployment to ensure that the best use of HR services is being made.

OPERATIONAL MANAGEMENT MEETINGS – SSC

Operational management meetings should be a combination of both informal daily status updates and more formalised weekly review meetings between members of relevant teams. These meetings should focus on the effectiveness and efficiency of the relevant service, how this can be improved and a targeted review of current activity and resulting risks and issues.

SERVICE LINE MEETINGS – SSC

The management of the shared services operation will be responsible for developing a meeting regime that responds to the business needs. In principle, this will take the form of weekly or (minimum) fortnightly meetings to:

- Review operational performance and KPIs.

- Consolidate the service updates from across the HR SSC, identify changes or enhancements that will require agreement from the Service and Customer forum.

- Manage issues and resolution – those that cannot be resolved within the HRSSC will be formally escalated to the Service and Customer Forum.

- Resolve escalated complaints.

- Plan capacity and respond to peaks and troughs in demand.

- Review performance and service levels of third party providers.

- Address issues relating to resourcing the HRSSC, individual performance management, personal development and succession planning.

- Address all the other usual management requirements.

The principal output from these meetings should be an Operational Report that forms the basis of the input to the HR SSC operational meeting.

SERVICE MANAGEMENT FRAMEWORK

The Service Management Framework aligns the goals and objectives of the HR operation with its actions in terms of delivery against these objectives.

On its own the Service Management Framework will not guarantee successful delivery, but making sure that the framework is used and monitored and reviewed, through the governance structure described earlier, will provide the sponsoring Business Units with a flexible, scaleable HR service delivered consistently throughout the organization.

Figure 8.2 shows an example of a typical Service Management Framework with its various components and tools.

The Framework, if successfully applied, should create:

- A customer focused HR culture.

- An efficient mechanism through which performance against agreed service levels can be managed and non-performance escalated as necessary.

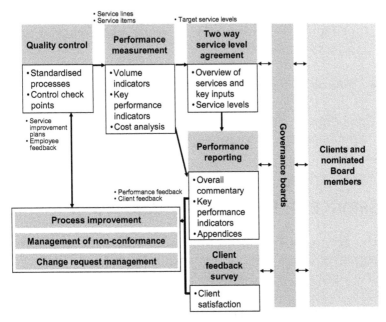

Figure 8.2   Example – Service Management Framework

- A focus on service performance and a continuous improvement mindset.

- Principles of Service Measurement.

There are a number of key principles for measuring HR's performance.

SERVICE LEVEL AGREEMENT (SLA)

The services and performance targets will be agreed with customers in a new Service Level Agreement. It will contain details of the standard and non-standard services (for example, some that are only provided to an individual business unit) provided and will document the responsibilities of HR and its customers. The SLA will be used to monitor and measure the effectiveness of service provision and its design is dependant on:

- Business agreement;

- Detailed process design;

- Understanding of the technology that will be used to support the service.

KEY PERFORMANCE INDICATORS (KPIS)

The SLA will contain Key Performance Indicators as an objective measure of efficiency, effectiveness, quality and customer service delivery. In most instances, KPIs focus on resolution times, data quality issues and failure/error rates for core activities. In the most sophisticated of shared services operations, service availability, customer orientation and the competence of SSC advisory team members will also be tracked. The key underlying principles are:

- KPIs will be calculated using standard pre-agreed formulae.

- KPIs will be based on objective evidence collected from the HR system, the Workflow system, the Customer Relationship Management system and the ACD (telephony) system.

- Relevant and pre-agreed 'live' KPI data will be published within the HRSSC that will demonstrate how targets are being met.

KPI data should be produced on a monthly basis and published as an assessment of performance against targets. The report should be tiered so that the appropriate level of detail is presented depending on the requirements of the recipient that is, the requirements of the HRD will be very different to that of a Team Leader.

BALANCED SCORECARD APPROACH TO REVIEWING PERFORMANCE

A balanced scorecard approach can be helpful as a mechanism for reviewing the overall performance of the HR function.

Category	Productivity	Customer Services
KPI	FTE per client record Workload per FTE Average transaction time	Call abandon rates Calls answered within x seconds Customer complaints Customer satisfaction index
	Cost per customer record Cost per recruit Cost per transaction type Total cost of service per employee	Accuracy of transactions 'Mystery Shopper' results Amount of re work
	Cost	Quality

Figure 8.3   **Outline example of a balanced scorecard for HR solutions**

QUALITY ASSURANCE

The Service Management Framework should have a Quality Control or Assurance element built-in. This will embed the concept of standardised and transparent HR processes and will provide the customer group with a degree of assurance that the integrity and quality of HR data and processes is being maintained.

CUSTOMER FEEDBACK

Customer feedback should be gathered on a systematic basis in order to determine satisfaction levels. These will provide a qualitative element to the Service Management Framework and should form part of the balanced scorecard.

SUMMARY

Any prospective HR transformation should consider five fundamental issues in the service design phase:

1. Start with service, not the underlying process. Know your internal customers and ensure that what you provide is what they need and can be integrated easily into their day-to-day work. However, beware tailoring service too extensively, only when there are genuine business needs to be accommodated or economies will soon disappear.

2. Don't be a slave to technology. The right technology will make life easier and your organization more effective and profitable, but 'over buy' technology and it becomes more than a long-term financial headache.

3. Manage the change. Your business is about to change in many ways and all of them should be for the better. This will only happen if you spend time, effort and hard cash ensuring that everyone from the very top of the organization down understands and buys into this change.

4. Establish the disciplines to run HR as a business by putting commercial service management disciplines in place.

5. Don't imagine you need to do all of this yourself. In many cases the lack of in-house expertise and sheer scale of the task at hand is a barrier to commencing the Outline Business Case and initial senior management engagement. There may be considerable benefit in calling on external consultants who have solid experience in this field and have a proven track record in delivering on all aspects of an HR transformation in an organization similar in scale, complexity or type to your own.

These success criteria can be applied at planning, implementation and post-implementation stages as they are underpinned by the principle that any effective HR service must be business led. They align the HR strategy and delivery strategy to the business strategy and are critical to ensuring a fit for purpose HR function that can measure and demonstrate the value it adds.

Orion Partners

Orion Partners are leading independent advisers in HR Transformation. Established in 2002, we have led and managed HR Transformation programmes for over 30 blue chip clients and our client base covers leading organisations in both private and public sectors.

We help organisations to succeed in their HR transformation by enabling them to:

- Clarify and define HR's strategy and role relative to the business.

- Decide on the most suitable operating model for HR, including the option of shared services or outsourcing.

- Select and implement the right technology solutions.

- Assess and select the right people.

- Develop the skills and mindset to succeed.

- Make the transformation happen on the ground.

Our unique focus is the whole range of HR transformation activities. We pride ourselves on the independence and practical nature of our advice and our focus on identifying and capturing the benefits in our design and implementation. We have skills and expertise in scoping, design and change management of the transition.

We have a have a broad base of functional, industry and global experience. Together with deep knowledge of HR and what makes it work successfully. We undertake regular research in the HR field including our unique studies on the difference that makes a difference in HR Business partners and HR Leaders.

If you would like to find out more, please visit www.orion-partners.com or call us on +44 (0) 207 993 4699.

GOWER HR TRANSFORMATION SERIES

This series of short books explores the key issues and challenges facing business leaders and HR professionals running their people management processes better. With these challenges comes the requirement of the HR function to transform but the key question is to what and how.

The purpose of this series is to provide a blend of conceptual frameworks and practical advice based on real life case studies. The authors have extensive experience in all elements of HR Transformation (having between them held roles as HR Directors and Senior Business Managers across a range of blue chip industries and been senior advisors in consultancies) and have consistently come up against the challenges of what is the ideal new HR model, what is the value of HR, What is the role of the HRBP and how can they be developed.

Whilst the guides all contain a mix of theories and conceptual models these are principally used to provide the books with solid frameworks. The books are pragmatic, hands-on guides that will assist readers in identifying what the business is required to do at each stage of the transformation process and what the likely options are that should be considered. The style is entertaining and real and will assist readers to think through both the role of the business and transformation project team members.

SERIES EDITOR

Ian Hunter is a founding partner of Orion Partners, a consultancy specialising in providing independent advice to organizations considering outsourcing their Human Resources department. He has worked for a number of leading management consultancies, including Accenture and AT Kearney and has been an HR Director in two blue chip organizations.

For Product Safety Concerns and Information please contact our EU
representative GPSR@taylorandfrancis.com
Taylor & Francis Verlag GmbH, Kaufingerstraße 24, 80331 München, Germany